Pebble® Plus

> DESTRUCTION <

SHRED IT!

by Thomas Kingsley Troupe

Consulting Editor: Gail Saunders-Smith, PhD

CAPSTONE PRESS
a capstone imprint

Pebble Plus is published by Capstone Press,
1710 Roe Crest Drive, North Mankato, Minnesota 56003
www.capstonepub.com

Library of Congress Cataloging-in-Publication Data
Cataloging-in-Publication information is on file with the Library of Congress.
ISBN 978-1-4765-2089-6 (library binding)
ISBN 978-1-4765-3490-9 (eBook PDF)

Editorial Credits
Erika L. Shores, editor; Heidi Thompson, designer; Marcie Spence, media researcher; Kathy McColley, production specialist

Photo Credits
Alamy Images: Chris Pearsall, 19, Jim West, 7, 9, 11; AP Images: Mike Derer, 21; Capstone Studio: Karon Dubke, back cover,
1, 5, 13, 15; Corbis: Construction Photography, 17; Shutterstock: Sombat Muycheen, cover, VectorZilla, design element

Note to Parents and Teachers

The Destruction set supports social studies standards related to science, technology, and society.
This book describes and illustrates the process of shredding tires and plastics. The repetition of
words and phrases helps early readers learn new words. This book also introduces early readers
to subject-specific vocabulary words, which are defined in the Glossary section. Early readers may
need assistance to read some words and to use the Table of Contents, Glossary, Read More, Internet
Sites, and Index sections of the book.

Printed in China by Nordica.
0314/CA21400181
022014   007226NORDF13

Table of contents

Shredding Time

The tires in the pile

are old and worn out.

Let's shred them!

A worker lines up tires
next to the shredder.

A tire is tossed onto

the conveyor belt.

It zips up the ramp.

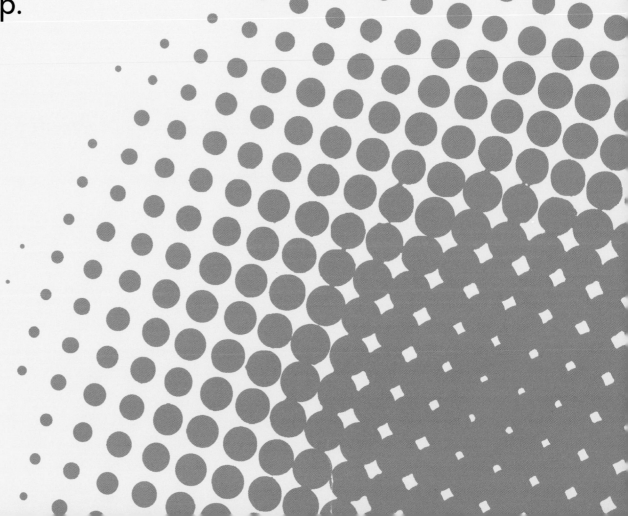

The tire drops into the shredder.
Whir! Crunch! Metal teeth
catch the tire and pull it
into the middle.

THUNK!

The metal teeth shred the tire to bits. Tire pieces fall to the bottom of the shredder.

The shredder has done its job.

Rubber chunks fall into a bin.

They are saved for later.

More Shredding

It's time to grind up
some plastic bottles.
Let's load the shredder!

The shredder tears up the bottles.

Tiny plastic pieces are all

that is left!

Shredded tires and plastic get recycled into new things. Rubber bits make a soft covering for playgrounds. Slides can be made from recycled plastic.

Glossary

conveyor belt—a moving belt that carries objects from one place to another

ramp—a slanted surface that joins two levels

recycle—to make used items into new products

rubber—a strong, elastic substance used to make items such as tires, balls, and boots

shred—to cut into thin strips or small pieces

shredder—a machine used to cut up objects into smaller pieces

Read More

Inches, Alison. *The Adventures of a Plastic Bottle: A Story about Recycling.* Little Green Books. New York: Little Simon, 2009.

Slade, Suzanne. *A Plastic Bottle's Journey.* Follow It! Minneapolis: Picture Window Books, 2011.

Weber, Rebecca. *Time to Recycle.* Earth and Space Science. Mankato, Minn.: Capstone Press, 2012.

Internet Sites

FactHound offers a safe, fun way to find Internet sites related to this book. All of the sites on FactHound have been researched by our staff.

Here's all you do:

Visit *www.facthound.com*

Type in this code: 9781476520896

Super-cool stuff! Check out projects, games and lots more at **www.capstonekids.com**

Index

Word Count: 138
Grade: 1
Early-Intervention Level: 14